16

Opening up schools for adults

Judith Summers

Published by the National Institute of
Adult Continuing Education (England and Wales)

21 De Montfort Street
Leicester LE1 7GE
Company registration no. 2603322
Charity registration no. 1002775

First published 2004

The *NIACE lifelines in adult learning* series was launched with support from the
Adult and Community Learning Fund, which ran from 1998 to 2004. ACLF was funded
by the Department for Education and Skills and managed in partnership by NIACE and
the Basic Skills Agency to develop widening participation in adult learning.

niace
promoting adult learning

NIACE has a broad remit to promote lifelong learning
opportunities for adults. NIACE works to develop
increased participation in education and training,
particularly for those who do not have easy access
because of barriers of class, gender, age, race,
language and culture, learning difficulties and
disabilities, or insufficient financial resources.

www.niace.org.uk

Cataloguing in Publication Data
A CIP record of this title is available from the British Library

Designed and typeset by Boldface
Printed in Great Britain by Russell Press, Nottingham

ISBN 1 86201 192 3

Contents

1 Schools and adult learners – the context for change   1
2 Partners   5
3 Involving parents, learners and communities   12
4 People   15
5 Funding   17
6 The offer   20
7 How do we know it is working?   23
8 Spreading the word   26
   Check it out   28
   Glossary   35
   Further reading and resources   38
   Useful contacts and websites   39

Note to the reader

Inspirations: refer to case studies and examples of good practice.
Glossary: the meanings of the words underlined in the text can be
found in the glossary on page 35.

Note to readers in Wales, Scotland and Northern Ireland: some of the
contextual information in the *Lifeline*, including policies for 'extended
schools', applies only in England. However, the role of the school in the
community is being re-examined and developed throughout the UK and the
principles and practical advice can be applied in most contexts.

Acknowledgements

This *Lifeline* draws on contributions and discussion at three NIACE regional conferences in December 2003, and the help of participants is gratefully acknowledged. Lenford White of NIACE has helped with advice and examples.

1 Schools and adult learners – the context for change

Schools matter for adult learners!

- There is a long tradition of using them as venues for both formal and informal adult learning programmes, making them familiar venues for millions of learners;
- They are geographically accessible – and in some places the only significant public building;
- Primary schools, particularly, offer family learning and opportunities for parents to learn in their own right;
- In areas of poverty and social exclusion schools can help to overcome cycles of deprivation;
- Therefore, used well, schools can make a major contribution to the well-being of the whole community.

Recent government policy has created new frameworks within which adults can learn at school, and providers can meet the needs of more and different learners. But as inspection reports show, current practice also needs to be strengthened. This guide, therefore, is for managers and fieldworkers in colleges, local education authorities (LEAs) and their adult and community learning (ACL) services, family learning, and voluntary organisations who already work with schools or want to begin to do so, and for those in schools interested in developing their school's role.

The most important new ways in which schools can open up opportunities for adult learning are:

- specialist status for secondary schools, whose 'community' dimensions might include formal and informal adult learning;
- the work of Sure Start, Education Action Zones and other initiatives to develop parent education and family learning, and further opportunities for parents;
- local IT learning centres established through Excellence in Cities, funding for neighbourhood renewal, or UK Online;
- extended schools: the extension of schools' services to meet community needs, following the Education Act 2002. Each LEA will be funded for a coordinator to promote extending schools across its area;
- the full service school, which links children's services and the school to achieve a holistic approach to meeting the needs of both children and families. The

DfES is promoting this model of the extended school, with one located in a deprived neighbourhood in each English LEA. (The 2003 White Paper *Every Child Matters* which proposes integrating the work of education, health, social services and careers in the interests of children, also sees the full service school as a means to this.)

'Extended' – or, as some say, 'extending' – schools is the term which gathers all these ideas together. The opportunities and challenges are:

- to build adult learning into local strategies for extending schools;
- to look at the lessons from traditional practice of adults learning on school premises;
- to understand how adult learning improves school pupils' attainment through improving educational culture and parental support – but also that it matters in its own right;
- to develop opportunities which widen participation and contribute to community regeneration, rather than serving those who already benefit;
- to avoid piecemeal or inconsistent provision, through schools determining their own priorities or managing provision in isolation;
- to persuade schools and LEAs to make the most of the 'extended school' idea and to think about what being at the heart of the community could mean;
- to offer support and expertise to schools in understanding the learning interests of their communities, creating worthwhile programmes, and encouraging the real engagement of learners and communities;
- to build partnerships between schools and other players to create a coherent and dynamic structure of opportunity which is *sustainable*.

> **"In disadvantaged areas in particular, extended schools have the power to transform lives. Our aim is to see more schools at the heart of their local community, providing learning and cultural experiences for all and offering help and support where it can easily be accessed."**
> Baroness Catherine Ashton, DfES 2002

"Education makes a significant contribution to community regeneration, and not just through developing knowledge and skills. An open school also helps to build social capital – through being a place where family and friendship networks are developed…shared values and mutual respect are actively promoted…where more vulnerable parents and pupils can feel safe enough to go for help. Add to this the job and career opportunities a local school can provide, and the facilities it can share, and it is clear that no other public institution carries such a heady mix of responsibilities and opportunities for community well-being"
Liz Allen, 2002

"Each extended school is unique in a unique local context… Think big, be bold, take calculated risks."
High School Headteacher

Photo: Creativity Works

INSPIRATIONS

Flegg High School, Norfolk

Flegg High School's concerns are rural deprivation and apathy. It used an Adult and Community Learning Fund (ACLF) grant to research, try ideas and develop its rationale. The Flegg Centre was created as a Neighbourhood Learning pathfinder and a college/LEA ACL/ Careers/school project has also organised a programme in community venues. Members of the local community play a major part in the running the centre, alongside a wide range of agencies. Flegg has now got capital funding to become a business and enterprise college, with a new community wing alongside a sports hall which will be a community facility. The school has made a long-term commitment; the agenda is not only to extend learning programmes and advice and guidance for adults, but to think more widely about needs, for example organising a community car pool service to solve transport problems. The school has the same philosophy for both school and community work: building relationships; enabling learners to partici-pate in leadership; helping communities take informed decisions.

Mitchell High School, Stoke-on-Trent

Mitchell wants to be a focal point for its community on a large social housing estate with high levels of deprivation. Satellites in community houses run by the residents association have activities such as drop-in ICT, exercise for pensioners, Citizens Advice Bureau sessions and health services. Adults also join school classes and evening classes on the site. A learning centre with a crèche supported by **learndirect** is also open to school students. Local residents have become a good proportion of school employees, mainly in support roles in ICT, as mentors, teaching assistants, attendance officers, play-leaders. Mitchell aims to create trust between the school and residents – for example, the residents association holds school keys and locks up after evening classes – and to help adults feel at ease with learning.

2 Partners

Who 'owns' what happens on school premises? Formal responsibilities lie with the governors, and as section 1 shows, government advice now assumes that the school makes the decision about not only whether but how to extend. However, sharing ownership between partners is critical to success, for three reasons:

- Without a shared approach to local learning, individual initiatives may duplicate or undermine others' efforts, fail to offer routes for learners and not maximise chances for adult learners. There will be enough learners to go round if partners work together to create a coherent set of local opportunities.
- Schools need to call in expertise – to help set priorities, design programmes and the curriculum, create support systems for learners, find tutors, train staff, set up quality assurance.
- Sustainable funding will almost certainly depend on partners' contributions.

Essential partners who will need to work together from the outset are listed below in the box. The list is not complete: there will be other important local players. Terminology and titles may vary locally.

Who?	Why?
The school	• Governors are responsible for the school and must agree to use of the school site; they represent local interests and many are close to the community • School development plan should include any community objectives • Knowledge of local community and its needs, diversity of the school community • Networks including sponsors, faith organisations, partner schools • Bring in other existing users of the school site, eg joint use libraries or sports facilities, community users
LEA	• Must be consulted on extended schools proposals

Who?	Why?
LEA	• Promotes development via its own strategic planning and extended schools coordinator • Essential source of advice on practical issues – personnel, budgets, premises, health and safety, childcare • Links to other authority services which may identify needs or opportunities eg. children's services, community development, external funding
LEA ACL services, including Family Learning	• Development planning is expected by LSC to include increasing schools' role in adult learning • Family Learning is an important starting point for many schools – use the LEA service • Consultancy; expertise in planning and delivery • Access to networks of partners eg. Family Learning networks • Depending on local practice, may provide adult programmes on school premises, contract with others to do so, or fund the school via a contract • Can access LSC capital funding
FE college	• Consultancy, expertise in planning and delivery • May provide adult programmes or contract with the school to do so • Already established relationships for 14-19 age group or for adult training
Other schools	• Shared interests in improving learning culture • 'Family' of secondary school plus feeder primaries can work together to draw parents in • May be established relationships to build on, for example through specialist status or Excellence in Cities • Possibilities for service sharing, joint appointments
Voluntary/ community organisations (see below)	• Often close to communities and their interests • Particular interest in informal learning and capacity building • May be able to organise and fund suitable programmes

Who?	Why?
Local Strategic Partnerships (LSPs)	• Bring together local government, statutory agencies, voluntary sector, business and community interests to work together for community, economic and social well-being and create community strategies or plans – helps you to work with agencies outside education • Strategies include demographic profiles and learning issues • Likely to have Lifelong Learning forum or similar, bringing diverse learning interests together
Neighbourhood Forum, local regeneration partnership	• Similar role to the LSP at more local level • Strong focus on community regeneration • Some have local 'action on learning plans' • Involving community activists – can help to develop real community involvement in your plans
Sure Start	• Commitment to parent education, family programmes and supporting parents' learning towards employment • Working closely with nursery/primary education • Children's centres may be valuable location for learners
Learning Partnerships (LPs)	• Partnerships of all interests in lifelong learning across an area – funded through LSC but independent • Can advise on learning issues • Can network you with partners to help in funding and expertise, and with specialist sub-groups
Learning and Skills Council	• Primary source of funding for post-school learning outside higher education • Development funding (see local LSC plans) for set priorities (eg improving skills, widening participation) • LSC plans show learning issues and priorities • Schools already linked as LSC funds sixth forms • Strategic Area Reviews (StARS) currently looking at how local provision matches needs

National voluntary organisations with local branches which should be involved include the Workers' Educational Association, the Pre-School Learning Alliance and the University of the Third Age. There may also be local organisations, such as a free-standing adult education centre. But look more widely. For example, the local Council for Voluntary Service (CVS) will network a vast range of local organisations, many of which might work with you on learning for their members or beneficiaries, and the CVS itself may be interested in training for capacity building. In rural areas the Women's Institutes promote learning for their members. Housing Trusts have a social dimension to their work and may know of needs or have projects to which you could add learning value.

Business and trade unions should also be considered. Businesses are not only there to provide sponsorship: they may already have the community on their agenda – for example, football clubs which provide training for coaching, or have an IT learning centre. Trade Unions are concerned with the learning interests of their members and their families and friends and <u>union learning representatives</u> can inform you about these.

What does partnership working mean?

- You should consult local interests at the formative stage of your thinking. This may identify organisations who want to join in.
- You'll need to understand each other's missions and know how each other's plans align.
- For some organisations you will need to establish a contact point and bilateral working arrangements.
- You may need to join some partnerships (or locate your representative on them) and establish your commitment to their wider goals – eg. LSPs, Neighbourhood Renewal Forums or Lifelong Learning Forums.
- You will need a forum of core partners who are committed to working together on the particular activity. This does not only apply to new projects: an existing programme might be helped by establishing or renewing partnership arrangements, for example to improve feedback to a provider from the school community.
- Partners' responsibilities should be agreed from the outset. Is there an overall lead partner? Who will hold partnership working together? What written agreements will you need between partners?

Creating a partnership forum or 'steering group':

- An effective group will work together proactively from the start.
- It will deal with strategy, action planning, monitoring and evaluation systematically, rather than just trouble-shooting.
- You'll need to decide at what point you formalise steering arrangements, agree terms of reference, objectives, and an action plan – but also agree how you will remain open to other potential partners whom you haven't yet spotted.

- Your steering group needs to be made up of people close to the action, including volunteers, but to have a clear line of accountability to school governors and to decision-making bodies in other partners. Your steering group should include school governors in view of the governing body's statutory role.
- You may of course need more than one level – one model is a 'board' for overall direction and one or more working groups.

However, partnership does not involve formal organisations only. What of the community and learners?

"The issue is designing public services to match how users, not professionals, would like them to work."
Director of Education

"Learning Partnerships can help you understand the local landscape and make the right fit. We work to the aspiration that every school can in some way contribute as an extended school."
Learning Partnership Coordinator

"Further education colleges offer expertise, resources, funding and partnerships. They can't offer easy answers, quick fixes, unlimited funding without strings. "
College Community Learning Director

INSPIRATIONS

Hertfordshire County Council

Hertfordshire Children, Schools and Families Service has increased the number of posts in Community Teams whose role is to work with schools and other partners to develop community-based services, including adult learning, and established a part-time Extended Schools Manager post. The integrated nature of the service means that it can look at all aspects of extending schools. It is working not with individual schools but with two clusters in an extended schools pathfinder. In addition, it is surveying all schools to set a baseline for development. The community benefits by access to learning, resources, premises for health and social care services, and the opportunity to be involved. The Adult Learning Partnership has 10 local Learning Forums to bring partners together. For Hertfordshire, planning for learning does not mean prescription but working locally and collaboratively with schools, partners and services, with extensive dialogue, to build learning communities.

Blackburn with Darwen Borough Council

The Borough philosophy of schools being at the heart of communities is about a holistic approach. Children's centres (at all nursery and some primary schools) will include lifelong learning alongside health care, early years services and job support. Extended schools might look at supporting people in debt, with a financial literacy programme and a base for a credit union. The local authority's task is to be an advocate for learning, energise schools and share leadership.

SPIRATIONS

Knowsley Community College

The college has a team of outreach coordinators, with each partner school linked to one. Schools are the channel for expressing local interests in learning and the coordinators set up college-funded programmes, including events to draw people in such as 'pamper days', and deal with practical problems. They also work at the school gate and attend school events to involve the school community, and will all gain NVQ level 3 in Information, Advice and Guidance so that they can support learners. The college helps to develop the school workforce, by training community members as volunteer mentors and teaching assistants, and working with Edge Hill College for a locally available foundation degree in teaching.

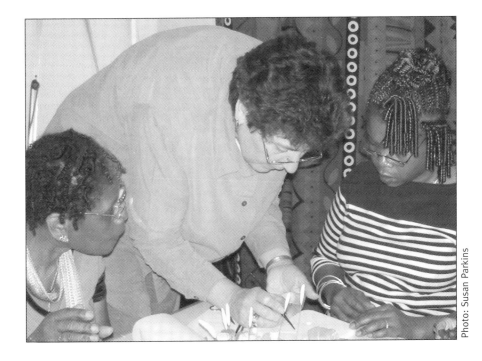

Photo: Susan Parkins

3 Involving parents, learners and communities

We need to involve both current and potential learners and their communities because:

- we need them to tell us what will work locally, how well things are going, what the barriers are and what needs to be changed;
- it would be perverse to organise learning as a contribution to transforming communities if we exclude the community from having a say;
- community backing is essential to sustainability;
- funding bodies and inspectorates require us to do so.

Parents' understanding and support are essential, whether or not they will be participants. Parents may be nervous about whether new activities detract from the school's attention to educating children, or about the dangers of more adults on site. They are entitled to be reassured. Governors are required to consult parents before deciding to provide any services and this is an opportunity to begin a dialogue about their interests. Existing means can be used, such as:

- newsletters
- parents evenings or school events with a stall to show plans and someone present to answer questions
- a homework exercise for children to seek their parents' views – number skills being practised in the analysis
- including questions in the school's parent survey
- getting the school council to prepare a presentation for parents
- parent governors hosting a focus group.

At the outset, reaching potential participants means hard work. The 'thinking it through' stage will enable you to decide whom you need to talk with and how. Written questionnaires are less effective than conversations which explore interests and start dismantling barriers. School-gate contact really does work! Education professionals may not be the best placed to do this unless they have both the time and the skills. You could consider:

- funding a member of staff to work on involving learners, but not necessarily a teacher – for example, an existing community liaison worker in the school;
- working through an intermediary organisation, such as an active parents' association, a community or residents' association, a disability group, local IT learning centre or trade union;
- recruiting, training and paying parents (who might already be helping in school or in out-of-school hours activities) or other members of the community to research interests, generate enthusiasm and be a learning advocate;
- convening a carefully facilitated meeting of potential learners, and using current learners to help. Exploit the interest of Adult Learners Week or a local event to help. Encourage local confidence by using local skills and if possible train community members to facilitate the meeting.

If you are building on existing programmes, there will usually be standard questionnaires for getting feedback from learners. But you may want to dig deeper and engage learners more actively. You could consider:

- periodic meetings of 'class representatives' (building on the WEA tradition) to find out their priorities for improvement and ideas for new activities;
- open meetings with hospitality, perhaps using Adult Learners' Week, perhaps linked to an awards event;
- using electronic consultation, such as inviting learners to vote monthly on an aspect of the service, or post comments.

Involving learners and the community is not just a first step or occasional activity but an integral part of opening up schools to more and different learners, and there are decisions to be made about how you will do this.

- How will you feed back the results of consultation to the community?
- Will there be learner or community representatives on your steering group? If so, what support will they get to make sure they participate fully?
- Is there a community group which should be a member of your partnership?
- How else can you involve the community in policy-making? For example, asking a disability group to provide expert consultancy on meeting the needs of disabled people?
- How can you involve the community in managing and organising activities?

See Lifeline 5, *Consulting Adults*, for advice on models of consultation and good practice.

"Our future health as a country depends on building active communities which support and serve the needs of all individuals within the community. "
Flegg High School

"If I started again, I'd have done more to engage parents informally – socialising before school events, personal invitations, getting them in, adding a bit extra, and asking them."
School Headteacher

"Don't use the term 'hard-to-reach. Recognise that all residents have a right to access learning, take learning to them, negotiate bottom-up. "
Family Learning Coordinator

"Recognise the importance of food and fun."
Primary school neighbourhood learning centre

4 **People**

One of the most frequently perceived barriers to extending provision for adult learners through schools is finding the time to do it. This is a particularly sensitive issue for teachers, and may also be for governors. Skills are equally an issue, although not always perceived as such. Partnership working should help tackle these problems, by releasing funds and energy from outside the school.

- The commitment of the school head (backed by the governors) is probably the single most important requirement for success. Unless adult learning is seen as integral to the school's objectives, provision is likely to be marginal and insecure.
- Once commitment is established, coordination might then be delegated to a senior school manager or a member of staff with an existing remit for community liaison or home-school work.
- The governing body may have an interested member with the time to contribute. If not, it could consider appointing an Associate Governor (ie. a governor appointed for this particular purpose, in addition to the current composition of the governing body) to help and maintain links between governors and the steering group.
- Parents or community members who act as learning advocates (see above) could be paid as organisers.
- There should be roles for volunteers, as with parent helpers in schools, some UK Online centres or in basic skills, but the rationale must be carefully thought out to avoid abusing goodwill, and 'job descriptions' agreed.
- Other core partners need to designate which of their staff will lead on a continuing basis, and to ensure that this person has the necessary authority.
- Be inventive: those with experience of extending schools emphasise the importance of innovation, rather than relying on existing models of who does what. Grow your own new workforce.
- Audit the skills available through all the partners and at all levels, both paid staff and volunteers. School governors and parents may have skills, for example, in publicity and promotion, which they can contribute.

Employment practices and culture will vary between partners. Practical issues to be resolved where new posts are to be created for a project, or if current arrangements are being reviewed, include:

- agreeing which organisation will act as the employer;
- deciding what pay scales and terms and conditions will apply – agreement and pay structures for support staff whether there are implications in the teachers' workload;
- school staff involved in additional activities can paid for working outside school hours (or given time off in lieu) – but you need to decide if this is the best solution, if staff have the expertise;
- thinking through line management responsibilities and support systems. For example, if the school employs a member of the community to organise new work, is it able to provide the professional support to help the worker understand adult learning and develop their own skills?
- Equal opportunities requirements apply to you as an employer – see details in Chapter 7.

Training for leading and organising the work will be an essential part of your action plan. Consider:

- using the 'Setting the Direction' checklist as the basis for a partnership training session, or to start identifying your training needs;
- what shared understandings you need to create – for example, valuing your community and its experience as well as knowing the difficulties;
- training on inter-agency working;
- visits to other projects or services (with a report to the steering group);
- short placements of staff or steering group members – for example, to learn how an effective IT learning centre runs;
- using your local college or adult and community learning service for advice on tutor training and qualifications, and for IT and other skills your staff and volunteers need;
- contacting the local Information, Advice and Guidance (IAG) partnership to set up training for front-line staff;
- capacity-building training offered through your local authority or the voluntary sector, to develop your management skills;
- making sure that volunteers are offered training, with the option of accreditation – it is part of what they get back.

5 Funding

Funding for continuity is the greatest worry reported by schools extending their services for adult learners. Schools may only legally use their <u>delegated budgets</u> for the education of their own pupils. Other sources available to them are almost always time-limited (although specialist school funding may be renewed after the initial four years). The government has made no additional funding available for extended schools other than the exemplar full-service schools in each LEA. Funding needs to cover not only delivery, but organising time. Funding initial research and experimentation is also an issue. There are, however, some solutions:

- seek small-scale development funding for the initial stages of research, setting up the partnership, working with the community and piloting ideas. This might be sourced from college or LEA ACL service development funds, from lottery funding (Awards for All), from local regeneration funding, or from other local partners. LSC funding for 'bite-size' activities (single, short learning events to engage learners) could also be used.
- different partners can access different funding streams – early thinking should review these and how they might be complementary.
- Long-term funding for adult learning is likely to come through partnership with an LSC-funded provider, usually an LEA ACL service or a college. LEA ACL services are expected to include in their development plans how they will work with schools to extend access for adults. The provider might contract with the school for the school to manage provision, or might 'put in' organising time and tutors. Sure Start is not time-limited and has an interest in parent/carer education, including training for employment.
- The school (and its partners) may want to discuss longer-term funding with the local LSC, in the light of funding for neighbourhood learning in deprived communities (if applicable) and in the context of <u>Strategic Area Review</u> (StAR).
- Fees: some adult learning provision in school will be free – either as a matter of national policy (remission of fees for people on benefit and their dependants; literacy, numeracy and ESOL courses or basic IT skills in UK Online centres) or because of local decisions about access for people in deprived communities. These apart it is prudent to set a fees policy and income projections, and not to assume that school-based provision will be at a cheaper rate than that

elsewhere. 'Membership' (with free attendance on some activities or a reduced fee rate) might also be useful.

- Recharging: if a partner is benefitting from use of premises or services, payment may be appropriate. Colleges or ACL services using school premises in the evening pay rent to cover premises, caretaking and cleaning costs. But equally, a school using services provided by a partner organisation should expect to pay, for example for using IT support from a community initiative on its premises. Recharging arrangements need to have a contract or service agreement, and external advice, say from the LEA, may be needed to determine apportionment.

- Income generation: through lettings or cross-subsidising activities: DfES guidance is that schools should take into account 'ability to pay' when charging for community activities. However, schools and their partners might agree to put on some high-income activities which could subsidise others.

You also need to know:

- If there are charges for provision or services for which schools are responsible, the Governors will need to agree the charging policy.
- Schools should establish separate budget accounts for additional services.

Photo: Susan Parkins

- Capital funding bids require specialist advice on what a particular setting might be eligible for.
- A fundraising sub-group may help you think widely, and prepare a coherent strategy for bidding for funds.

> **"We found we had to challenge existing practice – a provider who had previously used the premises for free needed to be charged now that the centre is separately funded and we need to generate income."**
> School Headteacher.

Bevendean Primary School, Brighton

Bevendean is in an area with limited community facilities and poor access. Starting with children's needs and the realities of parents' lives, it has put different funding streams together to create an interlocking programme of activities of which adult learning is a natural part:

- Parents and mother and toddler groups – funded by Early Intervention
- Health visitor clinic – funded by the Primary Care Trust
- Weekly Citizens Advice Bureau
- Family learning organised by the LEA – funded by the LEA ACL service, Sure Start and regeneration funding
- Breakfast Club – funded by New Deal for Communities
- After-school childcare – funded by the New Opportunities (lottery) Fund
- After-school clubs – children pay a small fee to outside providers, who pay the school a letting fee
- Adult education classes in the evening, with a crèche – provided by the further education college using LSC and LEA ACL funding
- Income from children's parties and other lettings which helps pay for the community manager.

6 The offer

There are no prescriptions about the curriculum to be offered. Decisions depend on what has been found about adults' learning interests and what opportunities are there to be exploited. Starting on a small scale, with pilots to see what will work and develop organisational expertise, makes sense but runs the risk of leaving provision isolated or fragmented. It's vital that the decisions about the curriculum are collective ones which put learners first and are not skewed by what it suits individual providers to put in. Some questions to consider about the curriculum are:

- What about the balance of activities? Are there enough informal and 'bite-size' opportunities, including learning fun days? If so, what happens next?
- Is there room to work with other neighbourhood services to create opportunities for informal learning and build on them? Examples might be access to IT through libraries ('Peoplenet'), or day centre activities.
- If there is provision already on site, is there scope for shifting resources to engage different learners respond to new interests?
- Are there activities which a family learning programme would naturally complement – eg. a crèche or neighbourhood nursery, or the school's parental involvement policy? What is the scope for this in secondary as well as primary schools?
- If family learning is already in place, how can it be built on or complemented?
- Is there scope for adult learning alongside holiday play schemes and summer schools?
- Literacy, numeracy and ESOL ('Skills for Life') have a high national priority: how can you contribute?
- If there are IT facilities, what is the curriculum vision for e-learning to go with them, and to move from learning to use IT to using IT to learn?
- What are the real challenges about progression? What will learners you have engaged be doing in two or three years' time? Do you need 'lateral' progression opportunities to keep learners involved?
- What about growing your own workforce – training cleaners, lunch-time organisers, teaching assistants, mentors, play leaders, sports leaders and coaches, and the many other adults employed on school premises?
- What about the curriculum for capacity-building – learning for local residents and community activists?

- Who will be responsible for providing appropriate accreditation and registration with examination bodies?
- How will you plan a rolling programme rather than working within traditional school terms?

The support available to learners is a crucial part of the curriculum, and you need a strategy at the outset, rather than piecemeal development, if you are to draw in new learners.

- Objective Information, advice and guidance (IAG) should be in place to help prospective learners make choices and current learners to decide about next steps. Partners should be able to cooperate to provide this service and the local IAG partnership can advise.
- Take the IAG to the learners. Community partners can provide locations for this. Look at training front-line colleagues in community organisations to give initial advice; it may be a natural extension of their role, although this may also raise funding questions for the organisation.
- Look at self-help and volunteering as means of providing support, for example 'IT buddy' schemes or user groups.
- Inexperienced learners 'moving on' to another setting are likely to need support through the transition – work with the Careers or IAG partnership to tackle this.

All aspects of what you offer must be planned in the light of legal requirements for access and inclusion, and should work positively to engage groups at risk of inclusion.

- Disability: how do the Disability Discrimination Act and Special Educational Needs impact on your plans? What local interest groups can you work with?
- Race: the Race Relations Amendment Act 2000 gives all public authorities (including schools) a responsibility to promote equality of opportunity and good relations between racial groups. Public authorities must have a written race equality policy and monitor the impact. How should this influence work with adult learners? Who will you work with?
- The Equal Opportunities and Sex Discrimination Acts continue to apply.
- Collecting data on your learner and staff profiles and matching it to the community's is not only a requirement but an essential part of your planning and quality assurance systems.
- Schools and their partners will have their own policy statements and arrangements for implementing them. Will you adopt one or do you need a new set for this provision?

"Lifelong learning policies which focus primarily on jobs are castles built on sand. Those that support existing networks and address wider social issues are most likely to bolster employment long-term."
Ian Nash, 'Go Local For Learning'

Sparkenhoe Primary School, Leicester

Hertfordshire Children, Schools and Families Service has increased the Adult classes for 2003/4 have included:

- Computer studies: New CLAIT; CLAIT Plus workshop; Text and Word Processing stages 1,3,4; ESOL Computers for Beginners
- Languages: Arabic (sponsored by the WEA); ESOL for new arrivals, beginners, intermediate; English conversation
- Food technology: cake decorating; advanced sugar craft
- Community lunch: wonderful Asian Cuisine (1 day); Hot Potatoes (2 days)
- Body and health: first aid for the home: first aid for the workplace; yoga; aerobics; keep fit for the less fit (GP referral scheme)
- Return to Learning: Maths – confidence with numbers; literacy with your child; GCSE English; Hawl Wadaag – learning together (women's group);
- Crafts and textiles: ESOL soft furnishings; ESOL through creativity; Asian pattern cutting; fun sewing with English; special educational-needs arts and crafts
- Evenings and weekends: laptop computers; Urdu for women; Chinese supplementary language school; complementary Somali classes

Crèche provided for all classes.

- Groups: Bengali women's group; carers, mums, dads and toddlers group

7 How do we know it is working?

All partners will be subject to external inspection or quality assurance (QA) frameworks which can be expected to involve collection of evidence and self-evaluation or self-assessment. ('Self-evaluation' is the usual term in schools, 'self-assessment' in colleges and ACL services.)

In the case of schools, the inspection framework asks how rigorous self-evaluation is and how well the findings are used. The school's self-evaluation is summarised in a pre-inspection form, but there are no other prescribed formats. Adult learning provision in schools comes into the framework, which asks 'how well does the school work in partnership with parents, other schools and the community?' and includes:

- the quality of any links with the local community – assessing, as appropriate, the extent to which the school provides a resource for and draws from the community; and
- the effectiveness of extended schools services and educational and support programmes for parents, families and members of the community (if included in the inspection specification) – assessing, as appropriate, the extent to which the provision is of high quality; meets identified needs; results in educational benefits to pupils and adults enrolled at the school.

Partners funded by the LSC are subject to a more complex regime of annual self-assessment as well as inspection by ALI (for adult learning), based on the Common Inspection Framework (CIF) principles. LEAs are subject to best value reviews. Voluntary groups may use the PQASSO – Practical Quality Assurance System for Small Organisations – Framework. UK Online centres have their own quality standards. In addition, project funding will have requirements for reporting outcomes and evaluation.

But self-evaluation has a number of audiences and should be organised and recorded in ways which recognise this:

- people working in the organisation, including volunteers – to improve their practice;
- those responsible for planning provision – to influence the strategy
- external funding bodies;

- governing bodies, college boards, local authority advisory or scrutiny committees, partners' steering committees or executives: to enable them to carry out their duties;
- external inspection or regulatory bodies;
- the community and the wider partnership network – who all need to know what is happening, to own and to value it.

Adult learning provision in schools therefore needs to lock into a number of QA frameworks, standards and reporting requirements. It is essential to understand what they have in common and to establish at the outset:

- what evidence the partners each require and how it will be collected and shared;
- who is responsible for providing evidence;
- what will be the self-evaluation process for the adult learning provision, who will lead it, who will be involved and when;
- who will use the evaluation and why;
- other ways than the formal reports in which you will present the evaluation – consider linking it to an 'annual report' which distils the messages.

But how do you judge success? Impact on children's achievements (a key Ofsted criterion) may be hard to judge, because cultural change takes time. Some schools working effectively with the community report increased pupil attendance and fewer exclusions. However, meeting numerical targets may tell you little. Many argue that you should take the initiative in elaborating the criteria in the inspection frameworks or developing your own ways of judging effectiveness and impact, particularly for innovative work linked to neighbourhood renewal. Examples which have been used include:

- how provision genuinely engages parents and members of the local community who have not been involved before (rather than those who already benefit) – through learner profiles and feedback;
- how parents value the school and its services more – through a parent attitude survey;
- how the community contributes to learning in the school – for example by providing learning mentors, or a drama group supporting school drama;
- evidence that the community values the school more highly – less vandalism;
- parents have greater confidence in their ability to deal with problems – shorter queues at the head's door;
- community members including parents have become actively involved in proposing new activities, leading and organising adult learning – and in evaluation;

- feedback from learners and users via focus groups;
- using different ways of recording learner's views and the impact on them - eg diaries, tapes, digital photographs, videobooths, electronic questionnaires and noticeboards;
- celebrating success!

"Often it will not be possible quickly to identify the precise extent of improvement or achievement brought about by community-based learning provision, at least in the short term – other than through the testimony of community members themselves."
Bob Fryer, 'Learning for the Twenty-First Century'

"There are two aspects to community education: engagement of the community to strengthen the work of the school; engagement of the school to strengthen the community. It is a two-way process and the second point is often overlooked."
HM Inspector

8 Spreading the word

Spreading the word serves many purposes:

- reaching potential learners;
- promoting the idea of learning (rather than just individual courses);
- keeping learners involved;
- helping the community to value you;
- being accountable to partners and to wider networks;
- engaging new partners and fund-raising;
- getting others going.

It is a good idea for the steering committee to create a simple rolling promotion plan which matches the different purposes to methods, for example:

Photo: Susan Parkins

- regular newsletters for learners and partners to build a sense of ownership;
- interactive areas on your website;
- using Adult Learners' Week to showcase your work;
- regular press/media releases;
- a lively annual report (see previous section), with pictures and quotations, which can be used to promote your work ;
- using school newsletters and its own annual report to parents;
- working with the Local Strategic Partnership or Lifelong Learning Forum to promote learning;
- creating a bidding prospectus – what do you want to do next and why, what do you need?

> **"Our over-50s group has taken responsibility for the newsletter."**
> Primary school neighbourhood learning centre

> **"The word on the street is that we are OK."**
> Head of extended secondary school

Afterword

The enterprise, vision and energy that has gone into these developments, often in schools in difficult circumstances, has perhaps not been fully appreciated. Fragmented funding opportunities have been seized upon and moulded into single visions by dedicated school, LEA and other agency staff. In this way, it could be said that extended schools ... have been a genuine 'grassroots', 'bottom-up' movement. A quiet revolution has perhaps indeed been in operation.
NFER Report, 2003

Check it out

Setting the direction checklist

This checklist can be used for school self-evaluation, for shared discussion between a school and other partners, or for consultancy to a school.

Understanding the context
- Why does the school want to be involved?
- What is the school's 'community'? Are there any particular groups which you feel are excluded or under-represented, which you want to work with?
- What do you know about the makeup of the community, and any significant economic, social, environmental developments? What are the issues which are relevant to learning? What do you need to find out? How will you find out?
- What do you know of the community's needs or interests in lifelong learning? How will you find out?
- How will you consult potential learners? Do you have any means of consulting the school community? How can members of the school community help?
- What learning opportunities are already available locally?
- What do you know about local structures and strategies – Local Strategic Partnership, Neighbourhood Forum, community strategies, local regeneration or rural recovery plans? Do they have any pointers for you – for example, identifying learning needs, potential partners?
- Are there any local strategies or networks which would help identify needs or provide partners?
- Who are the essential partners in developing, funding and supporting a programme for adult learners?
- What do you know about the local Learning and Skills Council plans and your LEA's Adult Learning Plan? What are their implications for you?

Understanding and building on strengths
- How are adults involved in the school or on school premises at present? Who is responsible for this?
- What experience is there to build on – for example, parental involvement, family learning, links with the community, out of school hours work, projects which could develop learning dimensions?

- Are there any points in the school development plan relevant to lifelong learning or other community activities?
- What resources are there in school which would help adults participate? For example: community rooms; suitable furniture; specialist facilities; IT suite; sports hall; suitable WCs; a crèche or space for one?
- Are there other initiatives at the school which could be built on?
- Which partners are best placed to do what?

Barriers
- What barriers could adults experience in accessing the school?
- What about access for people with disabilities?
- What are the barriers for the school – for example, security, pupil safety?
- What will happen in school holidays?
- Are there any legal constraints on how school premises can be used?
- How can these barriers be overcome? How can you make the school look welcoming?

Building capacity
- What are school governors' views on developing adult learning or other community activities? How will they be involved?
- What are staff views? How will they be involved?
- What skills and know-how have you got already and what do you need to develop? What are staff training needs?
- What expertise from outside the school will be needed?
- Within the school, who will be responsible for leading and managing development?

Ownership
- How will you involve the community in developing and steering activities?
- What formal partnership arrangements do you need to set up?

Success factors checklist

Factor	Features
Vision	• Purposeful • Clear and consistent • Forward looking and innovative • Learner-centred
Commitment	• Of partners • Of staff • Of school to the community
Joint Working	• Strategic commitment to joint working • Understanding it in practice • Working across the boundaries, outside the box • Community organisations and groups • Good communications systems
School Ethos	• Inclusive • Valuing the community and its views • Open access
Meeting Needs	• Developing around 'need' not tradition • Identifying and consulting with the community and learners • Support for learners
Location	• A focal point geographically • Outreach – going to the community and learners
Space	• Availability • Creative use • Accessibility
Flexibility	• Ability to accommodate changes to practice • Willingness to dispense with professional identities • Emergence of the 'hybrid' professional • Using the community and volunteers

Resources	• Capitalising on various funding streams • Good systems of procurement
Training	• Growing the workforce • For interagency working and building partners' capacity • For volunteers
Management	• Effective systems within school • Effective management between agencies • Clear lines of management responsibility • Sharing management roles • Including the community
Quality	• Building in evaluation from the start • Shared ownership • Defining how effectiveness and impact can be judged

(Adapted from a table in *Towards the Development of Extended Schools*.)

Photo: Susan Parkins

Practical problems A-Z

Access for disabled adults and meeting the requirements of the Disability Discrimination Act: Schools should have audited accessibility under the terms of the Special Educational Needs and Disability Act but may well not have been able to invest to meet all needs. A further access audit may be needed, with which a partner may be able to help, and minor capital funding may be available through the LEA ACL service or through partnership bidding to the LSC.

Attitudes: if the school is not perceived as welcoming, or indeed has not tried to welcome parents and carers, getting started will be a struggle. The first steps may be work by the staff and governors to review how they work with parents, and to build up informal contact, before moving on to more organised learning.

Costs to learners: may be a significant barrier – not only fees, but child and dependent care, materials, examination costs, bus fares. If a creche or neighbourhood nursery is part of the school development, it may be possible to arrange for learners' children to use it. A college or LEA ACL partner may be able to use their access fund to help with individuals' costs on provision they fund. Establishing a carers' group (working with Social Services) might enable you to plan provision to match care arrangements. Regeneration programmes may have scope for assisting learners financially. Discussion with the LSC on their widening participation strategy might lead to help for priority groups.

Child Protection and Criminal Records Bureau checks: apply to people, including volunteers, working with children and vulnerable adults, or having unsupervised access to them. Checks are made for schools through LEAs. Each school needs to make a judgement about other posts to which it might apply. For example, a tutor of an evening class for adults would not necessarily need a CRB check (although the organisers would consider whether the 'vulnerable adults' category applies), but a family education tutor engaged on intergenerational work might do. In the event of the CRB check showing a past offence, a judgement must be made about whether this is of a nature to make appointment undesirable. The requirement for CRB checks does not apply to parents or adult learners on school premises – but see 'Security' below.

Complaints: each partner will have a different set of procedures and learners, users and the wider public can be very annoyed if they don't know where to turn or feel the buck is being passed. You need to be clear whose responsibility it is to deal with complaints, and if possible to establish a single procedure. You also need to ensure that a profile of complaints and outcomes goes to all partners for their quality monitoring.

Health and Safety: school systems are not necessarily designed to deal with large numbers of adults, and partners responsible for delivery need to work together to understand their respective legal responsibilities, and carry out risk assessment. Examples of issues to be tackled are: health and safety induction for adult learners; ensuring there are sufficient first-aiders; arranging for incident reports to be reviewed by all relevant partners. Colleges and ACL services will have health and safety specialists who should help.

Insurance: schools need to ensure that their insurance covers new activities and opening hours and all partners need to check that there are no gaps in cover.

Legal status: the 2002 Education Act allows groups of schools to form a company for certain purposes. Some schools have also formed individual companies to manage extended activity. Advice must be sought from the LEA. Voluntary and foundation schools have charitable status and should check that proposals fall within their trust deed.

Numbers: imposition of minimum numbers requirements by established providers is frequently cited as a barrier. All partners involved in opening up schools need to accept that many activities will start small, and that relatively small groups are right for inexperienced learners. There is no solution other than for partners to understand this and agree to commit resources on a realistic basis, with an agreed rationale of how this can still show value for money. The steering group should discuss any proposals to close down activities because of low numbers.

Security: needs to be considered, if adult learners are on school premises during the school day and use rooms which are not separate from the rest of the school. A judgement must be made about levels of risk. Practical measures to help include: signing in at the entrance (as for all visitors); 'membership' with an ID card; a code of conduct for participants; ensuring teachers know what activities are happening where.

Site accessibility: adult users need parking, lighting for security at night, sign-posting. Local seedcorn funding may be available to help with this, perhaps linked to other improvements such as green space.

Staffrooms and staff facilities: staff may be understandably annoyed if adult learners or community members intrude into 'their' space. Be clear that staff need to have breaks, to work without additional interruption, and to have confidential discussions. Awareness is half the battle: negotiate what is acceptable. You may need to use capital funding, for example, for additional toilets.

VAT: schools should seek advice from their LEA (or the Specialist Schools Trust) and from Customs and Excise to ensure that VAT liability is not incurred.

Photo: Creativity Works

Glossary

<u>Adult and Community Learning</u>: refers to the learning opportunities, mainly informal, and including family learning, which are provided by LEA services and voluntary organisations and funded by the LSC. It may also be used to refer to similar learning provided in the community, which is not LSC funded.

<u>Best value</u>: local authority services are reviewed on a rolling programme with regard to their effectiveness and value for money.

<u>Capacity building</u>: strengthening individuals and groups to increase their ability to contribute to the life and well-being of their communities or to specific activities. This involves learning related to knowledge, skills and behaviours.

<u>Delegated budget</u>: the funding delegated to the school by the LEA under successive education acts

<u>Education Action Zone</u>: EAZ are self-managed partnerships of a cluster of secondary schools, feeder primaries, and supporting special schools, LEAs, business and community representatives, charged with creating new approaches to raising standards in disadvantaged urban or rural areas. Themes include family and pupil support. When EAZ end their funding they will become an 'Excellence Cluster' focussing on pupil attainment or an action zone within an Excellence in Cities locality.

<u>Excellence in Cities</u>: EiC is designed to address educational problems in the major cities. It focusses on secondary schools but in some areas includes primaries. Strands with a bearing for adult learners are learning mentors and city learning centres – ICT centres which are open in various ways to the community.

<u>Extended school</u>: a school that provides a range of services and activities often beyond the school day to help meet the needs of its pupils, their families and the wider community. (The DfES definition)

<u>Family learning</u>: parents/carers learning with or through their children, including learning to help their children to learn, and learning for their own development

Formal and informal learning programmes: 'formal' learning programmes are programmes with a planned content leading to a qualification or accredited outcome. 'Informal' programmes also have a planned content, often with some defined outcomes for the learning, but are usually more flexible and do not lead to a qualification.

Full service school: a school which is also the base for all services associated with children, including educational welfare officers, early years and childcare services, social services, and health professionals. The aim is to create a comprehensive service for children and families, with the school as the focal point, and a single point of contact for parents and carers.

Learning outcomes: what a learner has gained in terms of new knowledge and skills, or attitudes such as increased confidence. Learning outcomes may not be measured by formal assessment or testing, but less formally by tutor or learner self-assessment.

Neighbourhood Renewal means turning round the fortunes of deprived communities, with a combination of actions for social, educational, environmental and economic regeneration. Residents' active participation and role in managing developments are an essential part of neighbourhood renewal. New Deal for Communities is the major renewal initiative for the most deprived urban areas. Some rural areas have Rural Recovery plans.

Provider: an organisation which provides adult learning opportunities, eg a college, ACL, Workers Educational Association

Self-evaluation or self-assessment: the process of forming a considered judgement of the quality and effectiveness of the service, based on evidence. It identifies strengths and weaknesses and should lead to an action plan to tackle particular points. It should be used to guide development planning.

Specialist status secondary schools develop a specialism in one area in addition to the national curriculum, chosen from: technology, arts, sports, languages, science, business, maths and computing, engineering. They receive capital plus initially four years' revenue funding for this; one third of revenue must go to community dimensions of the specialism, which might typically include partnerships with primary schools or specific community organisations, as well as community access to facilities or adult learning. The term also includes technology, languages and sports colleges, which antedate 1997; these are similar and are likely to have a community dimension.

<u>Strategic Area Reviews</u> are carried out by all local LSCs as a planning exercise on the 'fit' between provision and the needs of learners, communities and employers.

<u>Sure Start</u>: is the national programme to improve children's start in life. Local Sure Start partnerships bring together early education, childcare, health and family support services; activities include parent/carer education and family learning, and supporting parents towards employment.

<u>Sustainability</u>: putting in place the resources, knowledge, skills and commitment to enable work to continue into the future.

<u>UK Online</u>: UK Online is the portal to UK government services. UK Online Centres are intended to enable access to email and the Internet for all; they are in disadvantaged localities or areas where access is difficult.

<u>Union learning representatives</u>: elected by trade union members to promote learning, union learning reps now have statutory recognition. Contact them via TUC Learning Services (see under contacts).

Photo: Creativity Works

Further reading and resources

Reading
- *Consulting Adults* (2003) Chris Jude, NIACE
- *Extended Schools: Providing Opportunities and Services for All* (2002) DfES
- *Childcare in Extended Schools: Providing Opportunities and Services for All* (2002) DfES and DWP
- *Inspecting Schools: Handbook for Inspecting Secondary Schools* and *Inspecting Schools: Handbook for Inspecting Primary Schools* (2003) Ofsted
- *Neighbourhood Learning Centres: Guide for Practitioners* (2003) DfES
- *The Learning Curve: Developing Skills and Knowledge for Neighbourhood Renewal* (2002) Neighbourhood Renewal Unit, Office of the Deputy Prime Minister
- *Raising Standards, Opening Doors: Developing Links Between Schools and their Communities* (1999) DfEE
- *Schools and Area Regeneration* (2003) Deanne Crowther et al, Policy Press for the Joseph Rowntree Foundation
- *Schools Are for Adults Too: Schools, Adults and Communities in the Learning Age* (2002) Judith Summers, NIACE
- *Schools Beyond the Classroom: Managing Collaboration for Social Inclusion* (2003) Liz Allen, New Local Government Network
- *Towards the Development of Extended Schools* (2003) Anne Wilkin et al, NFER

Resources
- *Building Learning Communities: Developing the Role of Schools in the Community* (2000) CEDC [now ContinYou]. This pack has valuable training materials and practical advice, although it antedates the extended schools initiative and is weak on partnership working
- *Learning for the Future: Neighbourhood Renewal through Adult and Community Learning* (2003) Bryan Merton, Cheryl Turner, Jane Ward, Lenford White, NIACE. This guide is produced for local authority services but could be used for shared development work by schools and their partners NIACE/LSDA.
- Adult and Community Learning Quality Support Programme publications, including *Fit for Purpose: Self-Assessment for Small Providers* (2002) Mark Ravenhall, Juliet Merrifield & Sue Gardener; *Self-Assessment and Development Planning* (2002) Mike Kenway & Anna Reisenberger. Learning & Skills Development Agency.

- *Neighbourhood Learning Centres: Guide for Practitioners* (2003) DfES
- *Talking it Through: a Practitioners' Guide to Consulting Adults in Adult and Community Learning* (2003) Sue Duffen & Jane Thompson, NIACE
- *Walking Ten Feet Tall: a Toolkit for Family Learning Practitioners* (2001) Jeanne Haggart, NIACE

Useful contacts and websites

- www.ali.gov.uk Adult Learning Inspectorate: common inspection framework and inspection framework for adult learning; reports of inspections of LEA ACL services and other adult learning providers
- www.awardsforall.org.uk Awards for All is lottery funding of up to £5000 for community activities, for which schools or voluntary organisations can bid; eligible activities include education
- www.continyou.org.uk ContinYou provides the Extended Schools Support Service (TESSS), funded by DfES to provide professional and technical advice, support and training for extended schools. email: extended.schools @continyou.org.uk ContinYou also organises a Community Schools Network and advises on developing out-of-school-hours activities.
- www.cre.gov.uk Commission for Racial Equality, for advice on implementing the Race Relations Acts and good practice
- www.dfes.gov.uk Department for Education and Skills
- www.dfes.gov.uk/ukonlinecentres Information about UK Online Centres – see glossary
- www.drc-gb.org Disability Rights Commission, for advice on Disability Discrimination Act and codes of practice
- www.governornet.gov.uk Governornet is the portal for information for school governors. Governorline 0800 722181 is the helpline for governors
- www.learningservices.org.uk TUC Learning Services, for information on trade union learning representatives and their work, and local links
- www.lga.gov.uk Local Government Association, for information on pathfinder extended schools projects
- www.lsc.gov.uk Learning and Skills Council, including links to local LSCs
- www.niace.org.uk NIACE
- www.nof.org.uk New Opportunities Fund – bidding opportunities connected to sports or childcare in schools
- www.ofsted.gov.uk Ofsted: for school inspection frameworks, and reports which provide useful pointers.
- www.skills.org.uk Neighbourhood Learning in Disadvantaged Communities information on policies and practice, linked to the National Strategy for Neighbourhood Renewal

- www.surestart.gov.uk Sure Start – information on all programmes, including local partnerships
- www.tct.trust.org.uk Specialist Schools Trust – information on specialist schools and their work, including search for individual schools
- www.teachernet.gov.uk/wholeschool/extendedschools Teachernet is a DfES site to support schools: the extended schools pages have guidance, case studies, and an extensive list of useful contacts. Other areas of Teachernet give guidance on school management, charging, premises, health and safety, disclosure and other relevant issues.

Photo: Creativity Works

Opening up schools for adults

NIACE lifelines in adult learning

The *NIACE lifelines in adult learning* series provides straightforward background and information, accessible know-how and useful examples of good practice for all practitioners involved in adult and community learning. Focusing in turn on different areas of adult learning these guides are an essential part of every practitioner's toolkit.

1. **Community education and neighbourhood renewal** – Jane Thompson, ISBN 1 86201 139 7
2. **Spreading the word: reaching out to new learners** – Veronica McGivney, ISBN 1 86201 140 0
3. **Managing community projects for change** – Jan Eldred, ISBN 1 86201 141 9
4. **Engaging black learners in adult and community education** – Lenford White, ISBN 1 86201 142 7
5. **Consulting adults** – Chris Jude, ISBN 1 86201 194 4
6. **Working with young adults** – Carol Jackson, ISBN 1 86201 150 8
7. **Promoting learning** – Kate Malone, ISBN 1 86201 151 6
8. **Evaluating community projects** – Jane Field, ISBN 1 86201 152 4
9. **Working in partnership** – Lyn Tett, ISBN 1 86201 162 1
10. **Working with Asian heritage communities** – David McNulty, ISBN 1 86201 174 5
11. **Learning and community arts** – Jane Thompson, ISBN 1 86201 181 8
12. **Museums and community learning** – Garrick Fincham, ISBN 1 86201 182 6
13. **Developing a needs-based library service** – John Pateman, ISBN 1 86201 183 4
14. **Volunteers and volunteering** – Janet Swinney, ISBN 1 86201 187 7
15. **Sustaining projects for success** – Kay Snowdon, ISBN 1 86201 188 5
16. **Opening up schools for adults** – Judith Summers, ISBN 1 86201 192 3

Forthcoming titles
17. **Befriending** – Jane Field,
18. **Literacy** – Mandy Lindsey,
19. **Numeracy** – Barbara Newmarch,
20. **ESOL** – Violet Windsor,
21. **Embedded basic skills** – Jan Eldred,